Unit 1

HOUGHTON MIFFLIN HARCOURT
School Publishers

Contents

We Camp

by Rich Rizzo

Sam can camp with his mom and his dad. Deb and Baby Cris can camp, too. They walked around.

1

Ann and her family camp. They get
in a big, big raft. They get wet. Ann
laughs lots and lots. Ann has fun.

Pam and her family camp. Kim and
her family camp. Pam and Kim grin and
clap hands. Pam and Kim can play.

Sid and her family camp. Sid can swim. Next, Sid can swim laps! Sid can swim fast. Sid can swim and Dad can clap for her.

Val and Kit camp with their family.
Kit and Val got Dad to snap some pictures.
Grin, Val, grin. Grin, Kit, grin. Snap,
Dad, snap!

Jud and Max and their family camp.
Jud and Max set up the tent. After it was
set up, Max sat and Jud sat.

Mat, Jim, Liz, and their family camp.
If Liz can zip past Mat and Jim, Liz can
win! Run, Liz! Run, Mat! Run, Jim!

Tim and his family did not camp.
They had a picnic at their house.

The Picnic Ants

by Kevin Carlisle
illustrated by Tom Leonard

Kim is an ant. Kim is a little red ant.
Tim is an ant. Tim is a big red ant. Kim
and Tim like picnics.

Tim had a tan picnic bag. Tim had
a red picnic mat and ten picnic napkins
in his bag. Tim had six plastic cups and
lids. Tim can go on a picnic.

Kim had a tan picnic bag. Kim had
milk, figs, ham, crab dip, mint jam, and
a big red yam in her picnic bag. Kim can
go on a picnic.

Tim sat next to Kim on his picnic mat.
Kim and Tim had sips of milk. Kim had
a fig. Tim had ham and mint jam. Tim
and Kim had good food.

Tim had a picnic napkin in his lap.
Tim can dab his lips. Kim had a picnic
napkin. Kim can pat her hands. Tim and
Kim dab and pat.

After their picnic, Tim and Kim
walked around. Tim and Kim saw Mat
and Pat. Mat and Pat saw Kim and Tim.
They all are glad.

14

Mat is an ant. Pat is an ant. Mat and Pat like picnics. Kim and Tim had a plan. Can Mat and Pat have a picnic with Kim and Tim?

Tim and Kim had figs, ham, and milk.
Tim and Kim had napkins and cups.
Kim and Tim, and Mat and Pat, had a
big ant picnic.

Bud, Ben, and Roz

by Melissa Rothman

illustrated by Jackie Snider

Bud and Ben plan a party for Roz.
Ben and Bud make lists.

Bud, Ben, and Mom get on a big
bus. Bud, Ben, and Mom sit on the bus
until the last stop. Bud, Ben, and Mom
get off the bus. Mom has the lists.

Bud, Ben, and Mom go in. Bud and
Ben get red bags. Next, Bud and Ben
get red cups. Bud and Ben get red hats.
Mom has their lists.

Bud and Ben set out red bags.
Next, Bud and Ben set out red cups.
Bud and Ben set out red hats. Bud
and Ben help set up the den.

Gus comes in. Deb skips in. Gus
and Deb sit with Bud and Ben.

Is Roz in the den? Not yet! Where
is Roz?

Did Ben get Roz? Ben did not get Roz.
Did Bud get Roz? Bud did not get Roz.
Did Mom get Roz? Mom did not get Roz.

"Mom! Mom! Can you get Roz and her family?" said Ben.

"Yes," said Mom. "I can get Roz."
Mom went to get Roz.

Roz is surprised. The children stand
up. Gus and Deb clap. Roz is glad,
glad, glad.

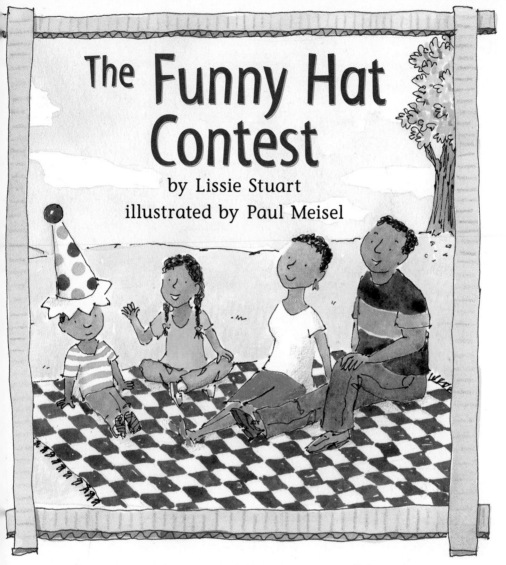

The Funny Hat Contest

by Lissie Stuart

illustrated by Paul Meisel

Gus and his family went to the Picnic
and Funny Hat Contest at Pumpkin Land.
Gus had red and tan dots on his hat, but
Gus did not win.

At the next contest, Gus had a funny hat. It had red plastic jets on it. It had red plastic drums on it, but Gus did not win. Gus felt glum.

Can Meg help Gus win the next hat contest? Gus can ask Meg.

Yes! Meg can plan and invent the best hat for Gus.

Meg got a big box. Meg got six red
dots. Meg got a plum.

"What is the plum for?" said Gus.

"I can eat it," said Meg.

"Gus, you can not see the hat until the contest," said Meg.

Gus left Meg. Meg sat and did her job. Meg began with the box.

Pat, pat, pat.
Snip, snip, snip.
Cut, cut, cut.

Children sit at the picnic. Meg comes
with a big bag.

"Open it up, Gus," said Meg.

The hat is as big as Gus. Gus got in it.
It is a funny hat.
Did Gus win? Yes, yes, Gus did.

City Ride

by Saturnino Romay

Ben and Ann ride to school on a big bus. Other kids ride it at the same time as Ben and Ann. Pals in Grade 2 sit with Ben and Ann.

Peg can ride up, up, up and can step out at the top. Peg can take time to gaze at the big city. Peg can step out and see it. Peg can ride down again.

Ed is late. Ed can get in a cab at the cabstand. The cab can take him to his job on time. Ed is glad. Ed must get to his job at six on the dot!

Gram came to see Kate and Mom and
Dad. Kate and Gram had fun, but it is
time for Gram to go. Gram is on the
plane. Kate, Mom, and Dad wave and
wave at the plane.

Jane and Ike like to slide. Jane can slide fast, but not too fast. Ike can slide fast, but not too fast. Jane and Ike can go up steps and slide down time and time again.

Nate can ride his bike in the city.
Nate can ride where it is safe to ride on
his bike. Nate and his mom and dad can
get on bikes and ride together. Nate has
fun with his mom and dad.

Ken and Roz like to skate. Roz can slide and glide. Ken can slide and glide, too. Ken and Roz can skate around fast. Zip, zip, zip! They can skate fast, but not too fast. Ken and Roz are safe.

Wade can sit on the same side as his dad. His name is Kent. Wade and Kent can take a safe bus ride to the other side of the city. It is quite a ride!

Mice Can Race

by Tatiana Rom
illustrated by Tom Sperling

This is Mice City School. It has six
grades. Cal is in Grade 2. His pal, Cid, is
too. Cal and Cid are in the same grade.

Cal and Cid sit at the same desk.
Their teacher is Dave Brace. He let mice
in Grade 2 call him D.B. Cal and Cid like
him a lot!

When he was in Grade 2, D.B. ran in the Mice City School race. D.B. ran fast and he came in first place! His prize sat by his desk. It was a big cup.

Cal and Cid ask D.B. if he can run a race with them and the other mice in Grade 2. D.B. can! D.B. can race if Cal and Cid find a nice race place.

Cal and Cid and their moms hunt for
a nice place. Cal and Cid find a fine
place to race. There is no other place so
fine. It can be fun to race here.

Cal, Cid, and other mice in Grade 2
stand with D.B. It is time! The mice get
set to run and win. GO!

The race is on! D.B. can run fast and
set a fast pace. Can Grade 2 mice run as
fast as D.B.? Can they get past him?

Yes!

The Grade 2 mice know that his prize
can be their prize, too. D.B. set the big
cup by his desk again.

A Bed of Roses

by Mira Carreras
illustrated by Nicole Wong

Zeke has a nice camp site. Zeke can
fix nice hot grub at the site. Zeke has a
nice home. It is a big red tent.

Zeke can get in his tent. His pals, Cate
the cat, Dane the dog, Peg the pig, and
Jude the mule, can get in the tent, too.

Today, Jude can help Zeke a lot. Zeke
can use a rope to strap his tent and pots
on poles. Jude can tote the poles.

It is time to set up camp.

"Stop, Jude!   Here is a nice place.

Let us set up camp here," said Zeke.

"Set up camp there," said Jude. Jude
saw red roses. Jude loved red roses. Jude
ran as fast as he could.

"Stop, Jude!" said Zeke. "Stop!"

Jude went on. Zeke and Cate, Dane,
and Peg ran after Jude. Jude did not stop.
Jude went on and on and on. Jude went
to the spot with roses.

Jude spoke up. "Let us vote," said Jude. "Vote 'yes' for roses. Vote 'no' for no roses."

Cate, Dane, and Peg cast votes. Roses won. Zeke gave in to the votes!

Zeke made grub at his nice new camp
site. Zeke put up his big red tent.
Jude and the cat, dog, and pig can rest
in a bed of red roses! Zeke did not mind.

Swim Like a Frog

by Chenile Evans
illustrated by Sonja Lamut

Meg is at Elk Lake Camp. Meg is in the big lodge. Meg is in the bunk next to Madge. Madge is the same age as Meg. Meg and Madge are pals.

Today, Meg and Madge can make bug masks. Meg can make big stripes on her bug mask. Madge can make big dots on her bug mask.

After crafts, Meg and Madge have a
picnic at the big lodge. Meg and Madge
eat slices of ham on buns. They eat
plums, milk, and pumpkin cake.

After rest time, Meg and Madge
can swim in Elk Lake. Madge has a
red cap. Meg has a tan cap. Madge
can swim and glide. Meg is just
learning. Meg must get help.

Meg can flip, flap, and flop. Her
hands and legs wig and wag, but Meg can
not swim like Madge can. Meg can not
swim at all. Meg is sad. Meg and Madge
hope Meg can swim soon.

Meg and Madge stand on a bridge.
Meg and Madge gaze at a big frog.
It can swim and glide just like Madge.
Its legs go in and out. Meg thought,
"Could I swim like that?"

Can Meg swim like a frog?

At swim time, Meg and Madge jump
in the lake. Today, Meg can see a frog
in her mind. Meg must swim like a frog.
Can Meg swim like that?

Fantastic! Meg did it! Meg can swim
and glide just like a frog! Meg can get
a red cap, just like Madge! Meg is glad.
Madge is glad, too.

Flint Cove Clambake

by Anne Miranda
illustrated by Adjoa Burrowes

Glen and Gram went to Flint Cove to
dig clams. Gram had made many trips
like this to get clams. Gram and Glen
had a rake, pot, plastic tub, bag, and a
picnic box.

Gram led Glen to the best clam spot in
Flint Cove. Glen dug. Glen slid his hands
in soft, wet sand and felt for clams. Glen
put ten little clams in his plastic tub.

Glen ran his rake in the sand.

"Not bad!" said Gram.

Gram bent to help him dig and probe.

Glen and Gram dug lots of clams.

Gram and Glen got water at a pump.
Gram made Glen spend time to get sand
off the clams. Gram had to scrape and
scrub them.

Gram and Glen got the big pot. Gram put clams, spuds, and yams in the pot. Gram and Glen set the big pot on a flat grate on the sand.

Smoke and flames rose up and the pot got nice and hot.

"It is time to set the table," said Gram.

Glen set out place mats, plastic cups, napkins, and plates.

Gram slid the clambake contents on a
big tin plate.

"Fantastic job, Gram!" said Glen.

"Fantastic job, Glen! Let us dig in,"
said Gram.

"Dad says clambakes are the best,"
said Glen.

"Let us save him some," said Gram.

Gram and Glen had a grand clambake
at Flint Cove.

The
Stop and Spend Sale

by Tyler Martin
illustrated by Cornelius Van Wright

Cran School has a Stop and Spend
Sale. It is in the gym. Fran set up a big
table. Stef and Stan will help. It will take
time to set it up.

Stan and Stef set a globe, vase, sled, craft box, and a little red plane on the table. Fran can make price tags. Fran makes scads of price tags, lots and lots.

Blake set up his table next to Fran.
Glen can help him. Blake had a bike,
camp stove, drums, and a kite at his
table. Blake and Glen made price tags.

At five, the sale is on! Moms, dads,
grandmoms, granddads, and kids come
in the gym. Stop and Spend stands have
hot dogs, clam strips, plums, grapes, and
pumpkin cake for sale.

Dane is at the table Fran set up. Dane
has five dimes. Dane spends his dimes
on a stamp. Deb has ten dimes. Deb gets
a plastic princess. It has a blond wig and
it says its name.

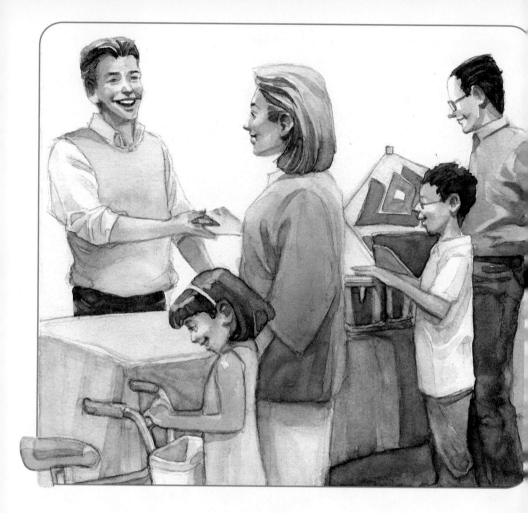

Mal gets the bike Blake has for sale. Bob gets the drums and kite. His dad got the camp stove.

Blake and Glen can spend a little time at the sale. Blake and Glen get hot dogs and plums.

The Stop and Spend Sale will stop at eight. It is almost time to stop, but Stan and Stef cannot stop yet. Just in time, Ron gets the red plane and globe. Steve gets six nice place mats. Fran, Stan, and Stef have nothing left. They can stop.

Stop and Spend
SALE

"The Stop and Spend Sale is always fun," said Fran.

"Yes, it is," said Blake.

"I am glad that I am a teacher at this school," said Fran.

Word Lists

Accompanies
Henry and Mudge

We Camp

page 1

Decodable Words
Target Skill: *Short vowels a, i*
and, Ann, at, big, camp, can, clap, Cris, dad, did, fast, grin, had, hands, has, his, if, in, it, Jim, Kim, Kit, laps, Liz, Mat, Max, Pam, past, picnic, raft, Sam, sat, Sid, snap, swim, this, Tim, Val, win, zip

Words Using Previously Taught Skills
Deb, fun, get, got, Jud, mom, not, run, set, tent, up, wet

High-Frequency Words
New
around, next, walked

Previously Taught
a, after, Baby, family, her, house, laughs, pictures, play, their, they, to, too, was, with

The Picnic Ants

page 9

Decodable Words
Target Skill: *VCCV pattern*
(with short vowels a, i)
napkin, napkins, picnic, picnics, plastic

Target Skill: *Short vowels a, i*
an, and, ant, bag, big, can, crab, dab, dip, figs, glad, had, ham, hands, his, in, is, jam, Kim, lap, lids, lips, mat, milk, mint, pat, plan, sat, sips, six, tan, Tim, yam

Words Using Previously Taught Skills
cups, on, red, ten

High-Frequency Words
New
around, next, walked

Previously Taught
a, after, are, all, food, go, good, have, her, like, little, of, saw, their, they, to, with

Ben, Bud, and Roz
page 17

Decodable Words
Target Skill: *Short vowels o, u, e*
Ben, Bud, bus, cups, Deb, den, get, Gus, Mom, not, on, red, Roz, set, stop, up, went, yes, yet

Words Using Previously Taught Skills
and, bags, big, can, clap, did, glad, has, hats, in, is, last, lists, plan, sit, skips, stand

High-Frequency Words
New
children, comes, family

Previously Taught
a, I, for, go, help, her, make, next, off, out, party, said, surprised, the, their, to, until, where, with, you

The Funny Hat Contest
page 25

Decodable Words
Target Skill: *Review VCCV pattern*
contest, invent, picnic, plastic, pumpkin, until

Target Skill: *Short vowels o, u, e*
best, box, but, cut, dots, drums, felt, glum, got, Gus, help, jets, job, left, Meg, not, on, plum, red, up, went, yes

Words Using Previously Taught Skills
and, as, ask, at, bag, big, can, did, had, hat, his, in, is, it, land, pat, plan, sat, sit, six, snip, tan, win

High-Frequency Words
New
children, comes, family

Previously Taught
a, began, eat, for, funny, her, I, next, open, said, see, the, to, what, with, you

City Ride

page 33

Decodable Words
Target Skill: *Long vowels a, i
(CVCe, longer words)*
bike, bikes, came, gaze, glide, grade,
Ike, Jane, Kate, late, like, name, Nate,
plane, quite, ride, safe, same, side,
skate, slide, take, time, Wade, wave

Words Using Previously Taught Skills
and, Ann, as, at, Ben, big, bus, but, cab,
cabstand, can, dad, dot, Ed, fast, fun,
get, glad, Gram, had, has, him, his, in,
is, it, job, Ken, Kent, kids, mom, must,
not, on, pals, Peg, Roz, sit, six, step,
steps, top, tram, up, zip

High-Frequency Words
New
city, other, school

Previously Taught
a, again, are, around, down,
for, go, other, out, see,
the, they, to, together, too,
where, with

Mice Can Race

page 41

Decodable Words
Target Skill: *Sounds for c*
Brace, Cal, came, can, Cid, cup, mice,
nice, pace, place, race

Target Skill: *Long vowels a, i
(CVCe, longer words)*
Dave, fine, grade, grades, like, prize,
same

Words Using Previously Taught Skills
and, as, ask, at, big, desk, fast, fun, get,
has, him, his, hunt, if, in, is, it, let, lot,
moms, pal, past, ran, run, sat, set, sit,
six, stand, them, this, time, when, will,
win, yes

High-Frequency Words
New
city, other, school

Previously Taught
a, again, are, be, by, call,
find, first, for, go, he, here,
know, no, so, teacher, the,
their, there, they, to, too,
was, with

A Bed of Roses

page 49

Decodable Words
Target Skill: *Long vowels o, u, e*
(CVCe, longer words)
close, home, Jude, mule, poles, rope,
roses, site, spoke, stove, tote, use, vote,
votes, Zeke

Words Using Previously Taught Skills
and, as, at, bed, big, camp, can, cast,
Cate, cat, Dane, did, dog, fast, fix, flaps,
gave, get, grub, has, help, his, hot, in, is,
it, just, let, lot, made, nice, not, on, pals,
Peg, pig, place, pots, ran, red, rest, sat,
set, spot, stop, strap, tent, time, up, us,
went, yes

High-Frequency Words
New
could, mind, today

Previously Taught
a, after, for, he, here, loved,
new, no, of, put, said, saw,
the, there, they, to, too,
with, won

Swim Like a Frog

page 57

Decodable Words
Target Skill: *Sounds for g*
age, big, bridge, bug, frog, gaze, get,
lodge, Madge, wag, wig

Target Skill: *Long vowels o, u, e
(CVCe, longer words)*
hope, jump, just

Words Using Previously Taught Skills
and, as, at, bunk, buns, cake, Camp,
can, cap, crafts, did, dots, Elk, fantastic,
flap, flip, flop, glide, ham, hands, has,
help, in, is, it, its, Lake, legs, like, make,
mask, masks, Meg, milk, must, next,
not, on, out, pals, picnic, plums,
pumpkin, red, rest, sad, same, slices,
stand, stripes, swim, tan, that, thought,
time

High-Frequency Words
New
could, mind, today

Previously Taught
a, after, all, are, eat, go,
have, her, I, learning, of,
see, soon, the, they, to, too

Flint Cove Clambake   page 65

Decodable Words
Target Skill: *Consonant clusters with r, l, s, including triple clusters*
clam, clambake, clambakes, clams, felt, flames, flat, Flint, Glen, Gram, grand, grate, help, place, plastic, plates, probe, scrape, scrub, slid, soft, spend, spot, spuds, trips

Words Using Previously Taught Skills
and, at, bad, bag, bent, best, big, box, contents, Cove, cups, Dad, dig, dug, fantastic, get, got, had, hands, him, his, hot, in, is, it, job, led, let, like, lots, made, mats, napkins, nice, not, on, picnic, pot, pump, put, rake, ran, rose, sand, save, set, smoke, ten, them, this, time, tin, tub, up, us, went, wet, yams

High-Frequency Words
New
little, says, table

Previously Taught
a, are, for, many, of, off, said, some, the, to, water

The Stop and Spend Sale

page 73

Decodable Words

Target Skill: *Consonant clusters with r, l, s, including triple clusters*

Blake, blond, clam, craft, Cran, drums, Fran, glad, Glen, globe, granddads, grandmoms, grapes, help, place, plane, plastic, plums, price, princess, scads, sled, spend, spends, stamp, Stan, stands, Stef, stop, stove, strips

Words Using Previously Taught Skills

am, and, at, big, bike, Bob, box, cake, camp, can, cannot, dad, dads, Dane, Deb, dimes, dogs, five, fun, get, gets, got, had, has, him, his, hot, in, is, it, its, just, kids, kite, left, lots, made, make, makes, Mal, mats, moms, name, next, nice, on, pumpkin, red, Ron, sale, set, six, tags, take, ten, that, this, time, up, vase, wig, will, yes, yet

High-Frequency Words

New

little, says, table

Previously Taught

a, always, come, eight, for, have, I, nothing, our, said, school, teacher, the, they, to, you